PIZZA NIGHT

60+ RECIPES FOR DATE NIGHTS, LAZY NIGHTS AND PARTY NIGHTS

Deborah Kaloper

Smith Street Books

BASICS

NEAPOLITAN

NEW CLASSICS

DEEP PAN

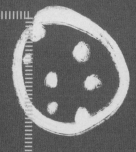

90

FRIED and STUFFED

112

SWEET

126

INTRODUCTION

Pizza – that perfect marriage of tomato, cheese and dough – is ancient history. The Egyptians, Romans and Greeks baked flatbreads topped with olive oil and spices long before 10-minute delivery was an option, but those flatbreads looked more like focaccia than the pizza we now know and love.

Naples was the birthplace of modern pizza, where early iterations were eaten by the lazzarone, or working-class poor, for centuries. Pizza was a poor man's dish that was simple and cheap to make. A mainstay of Naples' streets, it filled the worker's growling belly and was convenient to consume on the run, prepared with toppings like cheese, vegetables and anchovies.

In 1734, Naples created the Marinara (page 28). Topped with tomato sauce, garlic, oregano and a drizzle of extra virgin olive oil, it was the perfect dish for sailors who could easily store the ingredients onboard.

In 1889, the Margherita (page 30) was presented to Queen Margherita of Savoy, as legend has it, with patriotic colours that symbolised the Italian flag: red tomato sauce, green basil leaves and white mozzarella. Pizza finally transcended from a street food to a dish fit for a queen, honourable enough to represent a country, though it didn't truly sweep through Italy until halfway through the 20th century.

As Italians emigrated in the 19th and 20th centuries, they, as all cultures do, took their customs and foods with them. The fragrance of freshly baked dough began to waft through Italian neighbourhoods around the world, as nonnas baked up simple tray-style pizzas in their home kitchens. Much like Rome's classic pizza rossa, these simple slabs of dough were spread on baking trays and topped with tomato sauce, possibly scattered with cheese: easy to make, and large enough for the whole family to snack on.

In America, pizza's first home was New York City, where Lombardi's opened its doors in 1905 (which still remain open today). But it wasn't until after World War II, when returning troops sought out the dishes that they had discovered and loved while stationed abroad, that America's obsession with pizza really began.

The craze swept across the States, from New York to Chicago and Detroit to Los Angeles. Cities developed new styles of pizza, with unique flavour profiles and styles of doughs that locals claimed as the best.

Today, doughs vary from thin to deep pan, chewy to crisp, served as squares, rectangles and rounds with sauce on top, cheese on the bottom, or the reverse. Toppings are almost endless, and Californian-style pizzas are the most irreverent of all, with Tandoori chicken, surf 'n' turf, avocado and even vegan cheeses … definitely not Neapolitan!

Pizza Night's recipes feature a slice of pizza past and present, with something for every mood and occasion. If you're craving something classic, flip to the Neapolitan chapter for a Diavola (page 33) or slice of Capricciosa (page 34). For an adventurous night out, start with the New Classics and try Peach & goat's cheese (page 77), Spicy lamb (page 80) or Kimchi & sesame (page 83). When you've got a crowd to feed, dig into the Deep Pan options like the Grandma-style mortadella, burrata & pistachio (page 104) or the Chicago-style sausage pie (page 109). And for nights spent relaxing into the couch, the Fried and Stuffed or Sweet chapters have you covered, with Sopressa & olive panzerotti (page 114) or a Banana nutella calzone (page 132).

Learn to make your own dough, prepare sauces from scratch and enjoy playing with the very wide world of toppings, from the traditional to the pineapple. This book is for the home cook who loves to make and eat pizza, in all its incarnations.

Buon appetite, da mangiare!

PIZZA ESSENTIALS

Pan sizes	The recipes in this book are forgiving. If you don't have the correct-sized tray or frying pan, work with what's already in your kitchen; a few centimetres of difference won't make these pizzas any less delicious.
Oven temperature	Domestic ovens have different temperature ranges. To recreate the effect of a wood-fired oven, most recipes in this book require you to preheat a pizza stone at your oven's highest temperature. This will bake a perfect crust.
Pizza stone	Unless you have a wood-fired oven at home, a pizza stone is integral to home-cooked pizzas; domestic ovens have temperature limits, but pizza stones make up for the difference by absorbing and maintaining heat. This extra-hot surface creates a crispier crust for your pizza.
Pizza oven	You can skip the pizza stone if you have an electric pizza oven. These are a great at-home option; easy to use, they'll ensure you have a surface hot enough to cook a perfect crust without a traditional oven.
Pizza peel	Pizza peels make it easy to transfer pizza to a stone without any mishaps. If you don't have a peel, though, an edgeless baking tray or cutting board will suffice: dust with a pinch of flour, semolina or polenta and the pizza will slide right off.

KEY INGREDIENTS

Great pizza relies on flavourful ingredients: think artisan cheeses, extra virgin olive oil and fresh, local heirloom vegetables. Simple, seasonal produce bursting with flavour. The Italian style of cooking known as 'cucina povera' depends entirely upon the quality of ingredients used. As a result, simplicity is key, and less is often more.

CHEESE

Grana Padano	A hard, semi-skimmed cow's milk cheese with a grainy texture and a nutty, full-flavoured taste that's sweeter, milder and less crumbly than Parmigiano Reggiano. Produced in the Po River Valley, it is generally aged for 24 months.
Parmigiano Reggiano	Produced in the Parma, Reggio Emilia, Bologna, Modena and Mantua provinces, Parmigiano Reggiano is a hard cow's milk cheese with a sharp, nutty taste and savoury umami flavour. It is aged between 12 and 36 months.

Pecorino Romano	A hard, salty sheep's milk cheese produced in Lazio, Sardinia and the Tuscan province of Grosseto. Aged for 8–12 months, it is the star ingredient in the famous Roman dish cacio e pepe.
Gorgonzola	A blue-veined cow's milk cheese from the Lombardy and Piedmont regions of Italy. Gorgonzola 'Dolce', meaning sweet, has a subtle flavour with a creamy, lush texture. Gorgonzola 'Piccante' (spicy) is aged for longer, which results in bluer veins, a much stronger, pronounced flavour and a crumbly texture.
Fior di latte	'Flower of milk' is a mozzarella. Made from cow's milk, this fresh, semi-soft stretched-curd cheese has a sweet and mild milky flavour. Fior di latte has a more delicate taste and less fat than buffalo mozzarella, and is used as the base cheese in most traditional pizzas.
Buffalo mozzarella	Made from the milk of water buffalos, buffalo mozzarella has a creamier, softer texture than cow's milk mozzarella and a stronger, tangier, almost sour taste, adding another dimension of flavour to your favourite pizzas.
Burrata	Meaning 'buttery', burrata is a ball of cow's or buffalo milk mozzarella, with a curd and cream-filled centre. Usually eaten on its own or with fresh tomatoes, basil and extra virgin olive oil, it is a decadent addition when torn, scattered or melted atop pizza.
Low-moisture mozzarella	This mozzarella comes as a brick or block. Due to its low-water content, it is drier, saltier and denser than fior di latte or buffalo mozzarella. It is most often found on American-style pizzas, and never on traditional Neapolitan pizzas.
Wisconsin brick cheese	Named for its rectangular shape and origins, when bricks were used as weights to press and squeeze moisture from the curds. Traditional to Detroit-style pizza, this semi-hard cow's cheese has a sweet and subtle nutty flavour. It can be substituted on pizzas with cubed low-moisture mozzarella, which has a similar texture when melted, though brick cheese has a distinct flavour.
Bocconcini	Mozzarella balls the size of small eggs. Baby bocconcini are even smaller, like quails' eggs. They are usually made from a combination of buffalo and cow's milk.
Ricotta	Meaning 'recooked', ricotta is an Italian fresh whey cheese. It is made from the whey left over from the production of other cheeses. Similar to cottage cheese in texture, its curds are small, creamy and sweet. Ricotta can be made from cow, sheep, buffalo or goat's milk, and each has its own distinct flavour.
Mascarpone	Made from cream and citric acid, mascarpone is a smooth, creamy cheese originating from Italy's Lombardy region. Used in both sweet and savoury dishes, its tangy flavour is the perfect topping for a sweet pizza.

Pancetta

Pork belly that has been cured in a salt and spice mixture. Often cut into cubes or strips that are fried and added to pasta sauces, pancetta can also be purchased rolled and thinly sliced from delis. Just a few slices perfectly finish a pizza.

Prosciutto

Made from a hind pork leg that is cured with salt and spices and hung to air dry for a few months to a few years, prosciutto is typically sliced paper-thin and is used to top pizza with delicious results.

Mortadella

Ground pork – often combined with veal or beef – which is speckled with strips of fat, pistachios, peppercorns and herbs. Slices of mortadella look like a round, pink terrazzo tile.

Pepperoni

A classic, thinly sliced spicy pork salami with its own pizza flavour: the Pepperoni (page 36).

'Njuda

Unlike other sausages, which come in casing, this spreadable, soft and peppery pork-style sausage comes as a paste. A delicious ingredient for those who love spice.

HERBS

Basil

Known as the king of herbs and part of the mint family, basil can lift any simple rustic tomato sauce. With its intense green colour and spicy bright herbal flavour, it elevates the Margherita (page 30) with only a few leaves.

Oregano

Native to the Mediterranean, oregano has been grown and used in Italian cooking since Roman times. Another member of the mint family, its herbaceous flavour complements a wide range of vegetables, meat and seafood.

Rosemary

From the Latin 'ros marinus' meaning 'sea dew', rosemary is a robust herb that pairs beautifully with potatoes and crispy, salt-topped focaccia.

Garlic

This member of the allium family is pungent and spicy when used raw, but mellows in flavour and aroma when sauteed or roasted. The Romans regularly used garlic in their cooking, and it is a cornerstone ingredient in Southern Italian dishes, although it is used quite sparingly. Garlic clove sizes vary greatly, so use accordingly.

Extra virgin olive oil versus olive oil

Extra virgin olive oil is made by crushing olives to a paste and pressing (or spinning in a centrifuge) the paste to extract the oil without the use of heat or chemicals. It is the 'first press' of the olives and is often labelled 'cold-pressed'. The resulting product is far superior to regular olive oil, as the absence of heat allows the oil to retain its purity of colour, aroma and flavour. Extra virgin olive oil is a brighter green than olive oil. It has a grassy, floral taste and sometimes a peppery flavour. It must also have an acidity level below 0.08% after pressing to be classified as extra virgin olive oil.

Olive oil or pure olive oil is often a blend of olive oils containing various ratios of refined olive oil, virgin olive oil and sometimes extra virgin olive oil. It is much milder in both colour and taste.

Flours

00 flour is an extra-fine, soft wheat Italian flour often used for making pasta, pizza or breads. Using 00 flour results in a more refined and delicate dough. When using this type of flour for the recipes in this book, use 00 'pizza' flour.

Bleached or unbleached plain (all-purpose) flour is a multi-purpose wheat flour widely used in home cooking and baking, including cakes, breads, pastries and pizzas.

Bread flour is a wheat flour that has a high protein content, which helps to develop gluten. This results in a strong, elastic dough that will stretch and rise well when baked, for a perfectly chewy pizza.

Yeast

For consistency and ease, all dough recipes in this book use instant dried yeast. The granules are smaller than active yeast and do not require proofing or rehydrating prior to use in your recipe. Instant dried yeast works well with cold-proving doughs, which rise in the refrigerator.

Tomatoes

Fresh tomatoes from your garden or a farmers' market at the height of summer will always be superior to tinned, but these are only available for a short period. So when making pizza sauces, reach for the convenience and consistency of tinned whole tomatoes.

San Marzano tomatoes are a variety of plum tomatoes grown in San Marzano sul Sarno, near Naples, and are considered to be the best and most flavoursome tomatoes for making pizza sauce.

Anchovies

A staple in the pizza pantry, these small fish are usually packed in salt or oil, and are used for a punch of briny umami flavour. If using salt-preserved anchovies, rinse off the salt and pat dry before adding to your pizza.

Capers

Small edible flower buds from the caper bush. Tart and briny, capers add an indispensable burst of flavour that's especially good on a seafood pizza. They can be purchased pickled or salt packed. For the latter, rinse and pat dry before use.

NEAPOLITAN PIZZA DOUGH

BASICS

Makes 880 g (1 lb 15 oz) dough or 4 × 24 cm (9½ in) pizzas

500 g (1 lb 2 oz) 00 pizza flour or bread flour, plus extra if needed and for dusting

2 teaspoons caster (superfine) sugar

1¾ teaspoons fine sea salt

1 teaspoon instant dried yeast

320 ml (11 fl oz) lukewarm water

3 teaspoons extra virgin olive oil, plus extra for greasing

Notes: This is a high hydration dough, so it is wet and sticky compared to a drier bread dough.

Depending on room temperature, proving can take up to 4 hours.

Do not use a rolling pin to shape your pizza dough, as this will deflate it.

To use a stand mixer, attach the dough hook and combine the flour, sugar, salt and yeast in the bowl. In a separate bowl, combine the water and olive oil. Turn the mixer to low speed, slowly add the water and oil and mix for 2–3 minutes, until the dough forms a rough ball. Rest the dough for 1 minute, then mix for another 1–2 minutes, until a smooth ball forms. If the dough seems too wet and sticky (see Notes), add another tablespoon of flour and mix for a further 1 minute to combine.

To mix the dough using your hands, combine the dry ingredients in a bowl. Combine the wet ingredients in a separate bowl, then use your hands to incoporate the wet and dry ingredients together. Transfer the dough to a lightly floured surface and knead for about 8 minutes, until a soft, smooth dough forms, and shape into a ball.

Place the dough in a lightly oiled bowl, cover tightly and allow it to rest in a warm place for about 2 hours, or until doubled in size (see Notes).

Divide the dough into four equal portions. Using your hands, shape each portion into a ball and place on a lightly oiled tray, then cover and allow to rise for at least 3–4 hours, until doubled in size.

Alternatively, for a slow rise that will increase the flavour of the dough, follow the instructions above, but place the portions of dough in individual lightly oiled airtight containers, with room to rise. Seal and refrigerate overnight, or up to 3 days. Allow the dough to rise for 4–6 hours, until doubled in size.

SHAPING THE DOUGH

Sprinkle a work surface with flour, place a dough ball on top and lightly dust with a little more flour. Place your hands (see Notes) in the centre of the ball and push and stretch the dough out to a 24 cm (9½ in) circle. Take care to not deflate the air bubbles in the outer 1–2 cm (½–¾ in) edge, as these will create a beautifully aerated crust.

Your dough is now ready for topping and cooking.

FOCACCIA DOUGH

 Makes 1 × 23 × 33 cm (9 × 13 in) focaccia

500 g (1 lb 2 oz) bread flour, plus extra for dusting

2 teaspoons instant dried yeast

1¾ teaspoons sea salt

1 teaspoon honey

420 ml (14 fl oz) warm water

75 ml (2½ fl oz) extra virgin olive oil, plus extra for greasing

In a large bowl, whisk the flour and yeast together. Once combined, create a well in the centre of the mixture.

Dissolve the salt and honey in the warm water. Pour the mixture into the well, followed by 1 tablespoon of the olive oil.

Use a spatula or lightly oiled hands to mix the wet and dry ingredients together until they are completely incorporated, then shape the dough into a ball; it should be quite wet and sticky.

Place the dough in a large bowl, pour over 1 tablespoon of the remaining olive oil and roll the dough to ensure that it is completely covered in oil. Tightly cover the bowl and allow the dough to rest in a warm place for about 2 hours, until doubled in size.

Alternatively, for a slow rise that will increase the flavour of the dough, follow the instructions above until you cover the bowl. Allow the dough to rest in the fridge overnight, or up to 3 days. Remove the dough from the fridge and let it rise for 3–4 hours, until doubled in size.

Without removing the dough from the bowl, use a spatula or lightly oiled hands to fold the dough on top of itself a few times to deflate it slightly.

Grease a 23 × 33 cm (9 × 13 in) baking tray with 2 tablespoons of the remaining olive oil. It will seem like a lot of oil, but the dough will absorb it while baking, giving the focaccia a lovely golden, crunchy crust.

Tip the dough onto the tray and roll the dough in the oil until it is coated. Using your hands, gently spread the dough across the tray, stretching the dough evenly into the tray's corners.

Cover and set the tray aside in a warm spot. Allow the dough to rise for about 1 hour, until doubled in size.

Your dough is now ready for topping and cooking.

CHICAGO-STYLE DOUGH

 Makes 1 × 26.5 cm (10½ in) deep dish pizza

275 g (9½ oz) plain
(all-purpose) flour

2 tablespoons cornmeal

1 teaspoon caster
(superfine) sugar

1½ teaspoons fine sea salt

1½ teaspoons instant dried yeast

60 g (¼ cup) cold butter, cubed

140 ml (4½ fl oz) warm water

1 teaspoon olive oil, for greasing

Place the flour, cornmeal, sugar, salt and yeast in the large bowl of a food processor and pulse a few times to combine. Add the butter and pulse again for about 20 seconds, until the butter resembles tiny pebbles in the flour.

With the motor running, drizzle in the water and process for about 35 seconds, until a rough dough ball forms.

Lightly grease a large bowl with the olive oil. Shape the dough into a smooth ball with your hands, then transfer to the bowl, cover and allow to rise in a warm spot for about 2 hours, until doubled in size.

Punch down the dough, then shape into a ball again and return to the bowl. Cover and place the dough in the fridge for 1 hour, for the butter to chill.

Your dough is now ready for shaping, topping and cooking.

DETROIT-STYLE DOUGH

BASICS

Makes 1 × 25 × 35 cm (10 × 14 in) deep dish pizza

350 g (12½ oz) bread flour

1¼ teaspoons instant dried yeast

1¼ teaspoons fine sea salt

1 teaspoon caster (superfine) sugar

250 ml (1 cup) lukewarm water

1 tablespoon olive oil

Notes: If you don't have a Detroit pan, you can substitute a 23 × 33 cm (9 × 13 in) pan.

To prepare the dough for a grandma-style pizza, use a 25 × 38 cm (10 × 15 in) baking tray.

Place the flour, yeast, salt and sugar in the large bowl of a food processor and pulse to combine.

With the motor running, slowly add the water and process until the dough forms a rough ball, about 40–60 seconds. Tip the dough onto a work surface and shape into a disc.

Grease a 25 × 35 cm (10 × 14 in) Detroit pan (see Notes) with the olive oil, covering the base and side completely. Place the dough in the centre of the pan, tossing and turning the dough to coat it in the oil. Cover and allow the dough to rise in a warm spot for about 2 hours, until doubled in size.

Using your hands, stretch and push the dough into the pan's corners as much as possible without creating tears. Cover the dough again and allow to rise for 1–1½ hours, until doubled in size.

Your dough is now ready for topping and cooking.

FRIED & SWEET DOUGH

 Makes 800 g (1 lb 15 oz) dough

500 g (1 lb 2 oz) 00 pizza flour or bread flour

1 teaspoon instant dried yeast

1¼ teaspoons fine sea salt

1 teaspoon caster (superfine) sugar

250 ml (1 cup) lukewarm water

40 ml (1¼ fl oz) extra virgin olive oil, plus extra for greasing

Note: This dough makes enough for 16 pizzette, 10 panzerotti and 6 calzoni.

Place the flour, yeast, salt and sugar in the large bowl of a food processor and pulse to combine.

With the motor running, slowly add the water, followed by the olive oil, and process for 40–60 seconds, until a rough dough ball forms.

Bring the dough together and shape into a smooth ball with your hands, then place in a large lightly oiled bowl, turning the dough to coat it in the oil. Cover the dough and allow to rise in a warm spot for about 2 hours, until doubled in size.

Divide the dough into desired portions (see Note). Roll each portion into a ball, place on lightly oiled tray(s), cover and rest for 40–50 minutes, until doubled in size.

Your dough is now ready for shaping and cooking.

SAN MARZANO TOMATO SAUCE

 Makes about 500 g (2 cups)

800 g (1 lb 12 oz) tins San Marzano tomatoes

1 tablespoon extra virgin olive oil

3 basil leaves

Drain the tomatoes in a colander with a bowl underneath to catch the juice. Drain for a couple of minutes, then place the tomatoes in a separate bowl and save the juice for another use.

Crush the tomatoes into small pieces using your hands, then add the oil, basil leaves and a good pinch of salt. Stir together and place the sauce in an airtight container.

The sauce will keep in the fridge for 4–5 days.

MARINARA SAUCE

 Makes about 750 g (3 cups)

1 tablespoon butter

1 tablespoon olive oil

½ onion, finely diced

3 garlic cloves, minced

800 g (1 lb 12 oz) tins crushed tomatoes

2 teaspoons caster (superfine) sugar

1½ teaspoons dried Italian herbs

¼ teaspoon chilli flakes

Place the butter, oil and onion in a large saucepan over medium–low heat and saute for 5–7 minutes, until the onion is softened and translucent. Add the garlic and saute for 1 minute, until fragrant.

Add the remaining ingredients and simmer, stirring frequently, for 20–25 minutes, until the sauce is slightly reduced (see Note). Season with salt and pepper, to taste.

Let the marinara sauce cool completely before using on your pizza.

Place any left-over sauce in an airtight container and refrigerate. The sauce will keep for 5 days.

Note: If preparing the sauce for a Chicago-style pie, simmer for a further 5–7 minutes, until it has reduced and thickened slightly.

CARAMELISED ONIONS

Makes 360 g (1½ cups)

2 tablespoons olive oil

500 g (1 lb 2 oz) onions, thinly sliced

2 tablespoons balsamic vinegar

1 tablespoon brown sugar

1 teaspoon sea salt

2 small thyme sprigs, or ¼ teaspoon dried thyme

Heat the olive oil in a large frying pan over medium heat and add the onion. Cook, stirring constantly, for about 10 minutes, until the onion turns light golden. Reduce the heat sightly to medium–low and add the remaining ingredients, except the thyme. Stir thoroughly to combine.

Continue to cook, stirring occasionally, for about 25 minutes, until the onion is soft, darker-golden and tastes caramelised and slightly sweet. If the onion starts to stick to the base of the pan, add about 1 tablespoon of water and stir it through.

Reduce the heat to its lowest setting and continue to cook the onion for another 10 minutes, adding another splash of water if needed, until the onion is dark golden. Add the thyme and cook the onion for a further 10–15 minutes. Taste and season with more salt or balsamic vinegar, if desired.

Allow the caramelised onion to cool to room temperature, then transfer to an airtight container and store in the fridge for up to 5 days.

GARLIC OIL

Makes 250 ml (1 cup)

250 ml (1 cup) olive oil

8–10 garlic cloves, smashed

¼–½ teaspoon dried herbs, such as thyme, rosemary and/or oregano (optional)

Place the olive oil, garlic and herbs (if using) in a small saucepan over very low heat. Simmer for 20–25 minutes, until the garlic is soft.

Remove the pan from the heat and allow the oil to cool completely before transferring to a sterilised jar. Seal and store in the fridge for 7–9 days.

BASIL PESTO

Makes about 165 g (⅔ cup)

60 g (2 packed cups) basil leaves

**25 g (¼ cup) finely
grated parmesan**

2 tablespoons toasted pine nuts

2 garlic cloves

**60 ml (¼ cup) extra virgin
olive oil, plus extra for covering**

pinch of chilli flakes (optional)

squeeze of lemon juice (optional)

Place the basil, parmesan, pine nuts and garlic in the small bowl of
a food processor and blitz for 10–15 seconds.

With the motor running, slowly drizzle in the olive oil and process the
pesto to your desired texture (see Note). Taste and season with salt
and pepper, and add the chilli flakes and lemon juice (if using).

Transfer the pesto to a jar and pour a thin film of olive oil over the
pesto to cover. It will keep in the fridge for 5–7 days.

Note: Add an additional 60 ml (¼ cup) of olive oil to make a runnier pesto for drizzling.

LEMONY KALE PESTO

Makes about 375 g (1½ cups)

60 g (2 packed cups) basil leaves

**about 160 g (5½ oz) cavolo nero
(Tuscan kale), chopped**

50 g (⅓ cup) toasted pine nuts

2–3 garlic cloves

**50 g (½ cup) finely grated
Grana Padano**

**zest and juice of 1 lemon
(about 3 tablespoons of juice)**

160 ml (⅔ cup) extra virgin olive oil

Place the basil, cavolo nero, pine nuts, garlic, Grana Padano, lemon
zest and juice in the bowl of a food processor and blitz.

With the motor running, drizzle in the olive oil and blitz the ingredients
until combined. Season with salt and pepper, to taste.

The pesto will keep in an airtight container in the fridge for 5–6 days.

Note: For a healthier alternative, this pesto can be substituted for the basil pesto
throughout the book.

MARINARA

 Makes 1 × 24 cm (9½ in) pizza

1 large garlic clove, very thinly sliced

1 teaspoon extra virgin olive oil, plus extra for drizzling

1 × 220 g (8 oz) Neapolitan pizza dough ball (page 14)

80 g (⅓ cup) San Marzano tomato sauce (page 22)

½ teaspoon dried oregano

salt flakes

oregano leaves, to serve

Place a pizza stone on the bottom rack of the cold oven. Set the oven to its highest temperature (ideally 260°C/500°F fan-forced) and preheat for 1 hour.

In a small bowl, toss the garlic with the olive oil and set aside.

Following the instructions on page 14, use your hands to press, pat and stretch the dough ball out to form a 24 cm (9½ in) circle. Spread the San Marzano tomato sauce over the dough, then top with the garlic, dried oregano and a pinch of salt flakes. Finish with a small drizzle of olive oil.

Carefully transfer the pizza to the hot pizza stone and bake for 7–10 minutes, until the crust is golden and cooked through.

Finish the pizza with a few fresh oregano leaves and another small drizzle of olive oil.

MARGHERITA

 Makes 1 × 24 cm (9½ in) pizza

1 × 220 g (8 oz) Neapolitan pizza dough ball (page 14)

80 g (⅓ cup) San Marzano tomato sauce (page 22)

100 g (3½ oz) fior di latte, torn

extra virgin olive oil, for drizzling

basil leaves, to serve

Place a pizza stone on the bottom rack of the cold oven. Set the oven to its highest temperature (ideally 260°C/500°F fan-forced) and preheat for 1 hour.

Following the instructions on page 14, use your hands to press, pat and stretch the dough ball out to form a 24 cm (9½ in) circle. Spread the San Marzano tomato sauce over the dough, top with the fior di latte, sprinkle with a pinch of salt and drizzle with a little olive oil.

Carefully transfer the pizza to the hot pizza stone and bake for 8–10 minutes, until the crust is golden and cooked through, and the cheese is melted.

Top the pizza with basil leaves and, if desired, drizzle with a little more olive oil.

DIAVOLA

 Makes 1 × 24 cm (9½ in) pizza

1 × 220 g (8 oz) Neapolitan pizza dough ball (page 14)

60 g (¼ cup) San Marzano tomato sauce (page 22)

1 bird's eye chilli, thinly sliced

65 g (2¼ oz) smoked mozzarella or scamorza, torn

6–8 slices hot Calabrese salami

extra virgin olive oil, for drizzling

chilli flakes, to serve

chilli oil, for drizzling (optional)

Place a pizza stone on the bottom rack of the cold oven. Set the oven to its highest temperature (ideally 260°C/500°F fan-forced) and preheat for 1 hour.

Following the instructions on page 14, use your hands to press, pat and stretch the dough ball out to form a 24 cm (9½ in) circle. Spread the San Marzano tomato sauce over the dough and top with the bird's eye chilli and half the mozzarella. Layer over the salami and top with the remaining cheese. Season with a good pinch of pepper and drizzle with a little olive oil to finish.

Carefully transfer the pizza to the hot pizza stone and bake for 8–10 minutes, until the crust is golden and cooked through, and the cheese is melted and bubbling.

Top the cooked pizza with chilli flakes and drizzle with a little olive oil or chilli oil, if desired.

CAPRICCIOSA

 Makes 1 × 24 cm (9½ in) pizza

1 Swiss brown mushroom, sliced

½ teaspoon extra virgin olive oil, plus extra for drizzling

1 × 220 g (8 oz) Neapolitan pizza dough ball (page 14)

60 g (¼ cup) San Marzano tomato sauce (page 22)

80 g (2¾ oz) fior di latte, torn

50 g (1¾ oz) Italian Parma ham, torn

1 marinated artichoke heart, thinly sliced

6 kalamata olives, pitted

oregano leaves, to serve

Place a pizza stone on the bottom rack of the cold oven. Set the oven to its highest temperature (ideally 260°C/500°F fan-forced) and preheat for 1 hour.

Toss the mushroom and olive oil together in a bowl and set aside.

Following the instructions on page 14, use your hands to press, pat and stretch the dough ball out to form a 24 cm (9½ in) circle. Spread the San Marzano tomato sauce over the dough and scatter with two-thirds of the fior di latte and all of the mushroom, ham and artichoke heart. Top with the remaining fior di latte, the olives and a pinch of salt, and drizzle with a little olive oil.

Carefully transfer the pizza to the hot pizza stone and bake for 8–10 minutes, until the crust is golden and cooked through, and the cheese is melted.

Top the pizza with oregano leaves and drizzle with a little more olive oil, if desired.

PEPPERONI

 Makes 1 × 24 cm (9½ in) pizza

1 × 220 g (8 oz) Neapolitan pizza dough ball (page 14)

60 g (¼ cup) San Marzano tomato sauce (page 22)

80 g (2¾ oz) fior di latte, torn

1½ tablespoons freshly grated parmesan

50 g (1¾ oz) thinly sliced pepperoni

extra virgin olive oil, for drizzling

pinch of chilli flakes

basil leaves, to serve (optional)

Place a pizza stone on the bottom rack of the cold oven. Set the oven to its highest temperature (ideally 260°C/500°F fan-forced) and preheat for 1 hour.

Following the instructions on page 14, use your hands to press, pat and stretch the dough ball out to form a 24 cm (9½ in) circle. Spread the San Marzano tomato sauce over the dough and top with the fior di latte, parmesan and pepperoni. Drizzle with a little olive oil.

Carefully transfer the pizza to the hot pizza stone and bake for 8–10 minutes, until the crust is golden and cooked through, and the cheese is melted.

Sprinkle the chilli flakes over the cooked pizza and, if desired, finish with an extra drizzle of olive oil and basil leaves.

QUATTRO FORMAGGI

 Makes 1 × 24 cm (9½ in) pizza

1 × 220 g (8 oz) Neapolitan pizza dough ball (page 14)

1 teaspoon extra virgin olive oil

65 g (2¼ oz) fior di latte, torn

65 g (2¼ oz) ricotta, drained

50 g (1¾ oz) gorgonzola, crumbled

50 g (1¾ oz) provolone, sliced or grated

salt flakes

honey, for drizzling

Place a pizza stone on the bottom rack of the cold oven. Set the oven to its highest temperature (ideally 260°C/500°F fan-forced) and preheat for 1 hour.

Following the instructions on page 14, use your hands to press, pat and stretch the dough ball out to form a 24 cm (9½ in) circle. Lightly brush the dough with the olive oil and scatter the cheeses evenly over the top.

Carefully transfer the pizza to the hot pizza stone and bake for 8–10 minutes, until the crust is golden and cooked through, and the cheese is melted and bubbling.

Season the pizza with salt and pepper, and drizzle with a little honey for a delicious, sweet hit.

PROSCIUTTO & ROCKET

 Makes 1 × 24 cm (9½ in) pizza

1 × 220 g (8 oz) Neapolitan pizza dough ball (page 14)

80 g (⅓ cup) San Marzano tomato sauce (page 22)

4 basil leaves, torn

80 g (2¾ oz) fior di latte, torn

extra virgin olive oil, for drizzling

6 slices prosciutto

handful of rocket (arugula)

1–2 tablespoons freshly grated parmesan

Place a pizza stone on the bottom rack of the cold oven. Set the oven to its highest temperature (ideally 260°C/500°F fan-forced) and preheat for 1 hour.

Following the instructions on page 14, use your hands to press, pat and stretch the dough ball out to form a 24 cm (9½ in) circle. Spread the San Marzano tomato sauce over the dough and top with the basil and fior di latte. Season with a pinch of salt and drizzle with a little olive oil.

Carefully transfer the pizza to the hot pizza stone and bake for 8–10 minutes, until the crust is golden and cooked through, and the cheese is melted.

Top the pizza with the prosciutto and rocket and drizzle with a little more olive oil, if desired. Finish with the parmesan and enjoy!

CAPRESE

 Makes 1 × 24 cm (9½ in) pizza

1 × 220 g (8 oz) Neapolitan pizza dough ball (page 14)

60 g (¼ cup) San Marzano tomato sauce (page 22)

50 g (1¾ oz) buffalo mozzarella, sliced

8 cherry tomatoes, halved

4 bocconcini, halved

extra virgin olive oil, for drizzling

Basil pesto, for drizzling (page 25)

basil leaves, to serve

Place a pizza stone on the bottom rack of the cold oven. Set the oven to its highest temperature (ideally 260°C/500°F fan-forced) and preheat for 1 hour.

Following the instructions on page 14, use your hands to press, pat and stretch the dough ball out to form a 24 cm (9½ in) circle. Spread the San Marzano tomato sauce over the dough and top with the mozzarella, cherry tomato halves and bocconcini. Season with a pinch of salt and drizzle with a little olive oil.

Carefully transfer the pizza to the hot pizza stone and bake for 8–10 minutes, until the crust is golden and cooked through, and the cheese is melted and bubbling.

Top the cooked pizza with with basil pesto, to taste, and finish with basil leaves.

AMATRICIANA

 Makes 1 × 24 cm (9½ in) pizza

1 × 220 g (8 oz) Neapolitan pizza dough ball (page 14)

60 g (¼ cup) San Marzano tomato sauce (page 22)

½ garlic clove, grated

20 g (¾ oz) provolone, shredded

50 g (1¾ oz) fior di latte, torn

6 thin slices (about 50 g/1¾ oz) round pancetta

¼ small red onion, thinly sliced

2–3 tablespoons freshly grated pecorino

Garlic oil, for drizzling (see page 24)

chilli flakes, to serve (optional)

Place a pizza stone on the bottom rack of the cold oven. Set the oven to its highest temperature (ideally 260°C/500°F fan-forced) and preheat for 1 hour.

Following the instructions on page 14, use your hands to press, pat and stretch the dough ball out to form a 24 cm (9½ in) circle. Spread the San Marzano tomato sauce over the dough and top with the garlic, provolone and half the fior di latte. Add the pancetta, onion and remaining fior di latte, and finish with the pecorino and a good grinding of pepper.

Carefully transfer the pizza to the hot pizza stone and bake for 8–10 minutes, until the crust is golden and cooked through, and the cheese is melted and bubbling.

Drizzle the pizza with a little garlic oil, and if desired, finish with a pinch of chilli flakes.

ITALIAN SAUSAGE & CAVOLO NERO

 Makes 1 × 24 cm (9½ in) pizza

1 cup (30 g) shredded cavolo nero (Tuscan kale) leaves

1 teaspoon extra virgin olive oil, plus extra for drizzling

1 × 220 g (8 oz) Neapolitan pizza dough ball (page 14)

80 g (⅓ cup) San Marzano tomato sauce (page 22)

60 g (2 oz) fior di latte, torn

100 g (3½ oz) Italian pork sausage, casing removed, crumbled into small pieces

40 g (1½ oz) cambozola, torn

Place a pizza stone on the bottom rack of the cold oven. Set the oven to its highest temperature (ideally 260°C/500°F fan-forced) and preheat for 1 hour.

Toss the cavolo nero with the olive oil and set aside.

Following the instructions on page 14, use your hands to press, pat and stretch the dough ball out to form a 24 cm (9½ in) circle. Spread the San Marzano tomato sauce over the dough and top with the fior di latte. Scatter with the sausage, kale and cambozola, ensuring that the pieces of sausage are small enough to cook through during the baking time.

Carefully transfer the pizza to the hot pizza stone and bake for 8–10 minutes, until the crust is golden and cooked through, the cheese is melted and the sausage is cooked.

Sprinkle the cooked pizza with a pinch of pepper and drizzle with a little olive oil.

ROMANA

 Makes 1 × 24 cm (9½ in) pizza

1 × 220 g (8 oz) Neapolitan pizza dough ball (page 14)

80 g (⅓ cup) San Marzano tomato sauce (page 22)

80 g (2¾ oz) fior di latte, torn

1 teaspoon baby capers, rinsed and drained (optional)

extra virgin olive oil, for drizzling

6 marinated white anchovy fillets

oregano leaves, to serve

Place a pizza stone on the bottom rack of the cold oven. Set the oven to its highest temperature (ideally 260°C/500°F fan-forced) and preheat for 1 hour.

Following the instructions on page 14, use your hands to press, pat and stretch the dough ball out to form a 24 cm (9½ in) circle. Spread the San Marzano tomato sauce over the dough and top with the fior di latte and capers (if using). Season with salt and pepper and drizzle with olive oil.

Carefully transfer the pizza to the hot pizza stone and bake for 8–10 minutes, until the crust is golden and cooked through, and the cheese is melted.

Top the pizza with the anchovy fillets and a few oregano leaves, season with pepper, and finish with another small drizzle of olive oil, if desired.

PEAR, LEEK, GORGONZOLA & WALNUT

NEAPOLITAN

 Makes 1 × 24 cm (9½ in) pizza

2 teaspoons extra virgin olive oil

100 g (3½ oz) leek, white and pale green part only, sliced

1 × 220 g (8 oz) Neapolitan pizza dough ball (page 14)

80 g (2¾ oz) fior di latte, torn

50 g (1¾ oz) gorgonzola

12 thin slices pear

small handful of rocket (arugula)

12 walnut halves, toasted and chopped

extra virgin olive oil, for drizzling

Place a pizza stone on the bottom rack of the cold oven. Set the oven to its highest temperature (ideally 260°C/500°F fan-forced) and preheat for 1 hour.

Add the olive oil and leek to a frying pan over medium–low heat. Season with a little salt and pepper and saute for 3–5 minutes, until the leek is softened and just cooked through. Remove from the heat and allow to cool.

Following the instructions on page 14, use your hands to press, pat and stretch the dough ball out to form a 24 cm (9½ in) circle. Top the dough with the leek, fior di latte and gorgonzola.

Carefully transfer the pizza to the hot pizza stone and bake for 8–10 minutes, until the crust is golden and cooked through, and the cheese is melted.

Top the cooked pizza with the pear, rocket and walnuts. To serve, drizzle over a little olive oil and season with salt and pepper.

MUSHROOM, THYME, ROSEMARY & FONTINA

NEAPOLITAN

 Makes 1 × 24 cm (9½ in) pizza

3 teaspoons extra virgin olive oil, plus extra for drizzling

80 g (2¾ oz) mushrooms of your choice, sliced

1 teaspoon salted butter

1 small garlic clove, thinly sliced

pinch of thyme leaves

pinch of rosemary leaves

½ teaspoon lemon zest, plus 1 teaspoon juice

1 × 220 g (8 oz) Neapolitan pizza dough ball (page 14)

60 g (2 oz) buffalo mozzarella, torn

handful of shredded fontina

1½ teaspoons finely chopped chives

Place a pizza stone on the bottom rack of the cold oven. Set the oven to its highest temperature (ideally 260°C/500°F fan-forced) and preheat for 1 hour.

Heat the olive oil in a large frying pan over medium–high heat, add the mushroom and saute for 2–3 minutes, until beginning to brown. Reduce the heat slightly and add the butter, garlic, thyme, rosemary, lemon zest and juice. Stir to combine and saute for a further 1 minute. Season with salt and pepper, then remove from the heat and set aside to cool.

Following the instructions on page 14, use your hands to press, pat and stretch the dough ball out to form a 24 cm (9½ in) circle. Top with the mozzarella, fontina and mushroom mixture.

Carefully transfer the pizza to the hot pizza stone and bake for 8–10 minutes, until the crust is golden and cooked through, and the cheese is melted and bubbling.

Finish the pizza with a light drizzle of olive oil and a sprinkle of chives, to serve.

'NDUJA, CHILLI, ANCHOVY & CHERRY TOMATO

 Makes 1 × 24 cm (9½ in) pizza

1 × 220 g (8 oz) Neapolitan pizza dough ball (page 14)

6 basil leaves

80 g (2¾ oz) fior di latte, torn

handful of freshly grated parmesan

10 black olives, pitted

8 cherry tomatoes, halved

6 marinated white anchovy fillets

SPICY 'NDUJA SAUCE

60 g (¼ cup) San Marzano tomato sauce (page 22)

½ garlic clove, finely grated or chopped

1 teaspoon finely chopped bird's eye chilli

30 g (5 teaspoons) 'nduja

Place a pizza stone on the bottom rack of the cold oven. Set the oven to its highest temperature (ideally 260°C/500°F fan-forced) and preheat for 1 hour.

To make the spicy 'nduja sauce, combine the San Marzano tomato sauce, garlic, chilli and 'nduja in a bowl.

Following the instructions on page 14, use your hands to press, pat and stretch the dough ball out to form a 24 cm (9½ in) circle. Spread the spicy 'nduja sauce over the dough and scatter with the basil. Top with the fior di latte, parmesan, olives and cherry tomato.

Carefully transfer the pizza to the hot pizza stone and bake for 8–10 minutes, until the crust is golden and cooked through, and the cheese is melted.

Top the cooked pizza with the anchovy fillets and serve.

PRAWN & CHORIZO

 Makes 1 × 24 cm (9½ in) pizza

5 tiger prawns (shrimp), peeled, butterflied and deveined

1 tablespoon chopped parsley, plus extra to serve

1 small garlic clove, minced

small pinch of chilli flakes

zest of ½ lemon

1 teaspoon extra virgin olive oil

1 × 220 g (8 oz) Neapolitan pizza dough ball (page 14)

60 g (¼ cup) San Marzano tomato sauce (page 22)

50 g (1¾ oz) fior di latte, torn

6 slices cured Spanish chorizo

⅛ small red onion, sliced

1 bird's eye chilli, thinly sliced

Garlic oil, for drizzling (see page 24)

Place a pizza stone on the bottom rack of the cold oven. Set the oven to its highest temperature (ideally 260°C/500°F fan-forced) and preheat for 1 hour.

Place the prawns in a bowl with the parsley, garlic, chilli flakes, lemon zest and olive oil and toss to coat. Set aside.

Following the instructions on page 14, use your hands to press, pat and stretch the dough ball out to form a 24 cm (9½ in) circle. Spread the San Marzano tomato sauce over the dough and scatter with two-thirds of the fior di latte. Add the prawns, chorizo, onion and fresh chilli. Top with the remaining cheese and season with salt and pepper.

Carefully transfer the pizza to the hot pizza stone and bake for 8–10 minutes, until the crust is golden and cooked through, and the cheese is melted.

To finish the pizza, sprinkle over a little more parsley and drizzle with a little garlic oil.

FIG, GORGONZOLA & PROSCIUTTO

 Makes 1 × 24 cm (9½ in) pizza

1 × 220 g (8 oz) Neapolitan pizza dough ball (page 14)

1 teaspoon extra virgin olive oil

6 basil leaves

80 g (2¾ oz) fior di latte, torn

50 g (1¾ oz) gorgonzola, crumbled

2 small figs, quartered

3–4 thin slices prosciutto

honey, for drizzling

1 tablespoon chopped and toasted hazelnuts

Place a pizza stone on the bottom rack of the cold oven. Set the oven to its highest temperature (ideally 260°C/500°F fan-forced) and preheat for 1 hour.

Following the instructions on page 14, use your hands to press, pat and stretch the dough ball out to form a 24 cm (9½ in) circle. Drizzle with the oil and top with the basil leaves, fior di latte, gorgonzola and quartered figs.

Carefully transfer the pizza to the hot pizza stone and bake for 8–10 minutes, until the crust is golden and cooked through, and the cheese is melted.

Top the pizza with the prosciutto and drizzle with a little honey. Finish with the hazelnuts and a little black pepper, and serve.

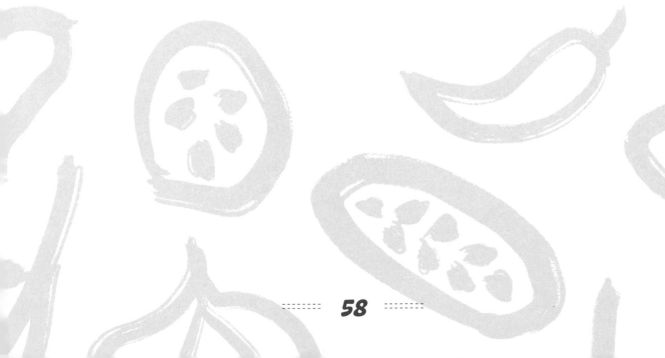

ZUCCHINI CARPACCIO *with* STRACCIATELLA & HERBS

NEAPOLITAN

 Makes 1 × 24 cm (9½ in) pizza

1 small zucchini (courgette), thinly sliced (preferably using a mandoline)

1½ teaspoons extra virgin olive oil, plus extra for drizzling

1 small black garlic clove, thinly sliced

squeeze of lemon juice

1 × 220 g (8 oz) Neapolitan pizza dough ball (page 14)

60 g (2 oz) fior di latte, torn

60 g (2 oz) stracciatella

shaved pecorino, to serve

1–2 zucchini (courgette) flowers, petals picked and torn

small handful of mixed herbs, such as basil, mint and chives

lemon wedges (optional), to serve

Place a pizza stone on the bottom rack of the cold oven. Set the oven to its highest temperature (ideally 260°C/500°F fan-forced) and preheat for 1 hour.

In a bowl, toss the zucchini with ½ teaspoon of the olive oil and half the garlic. Season with the lemon juice and a little salt and pepper.

Following the instructions on page 14, use your hands to press, pat and stretch the dough ball out to form a 24 cm (9½ in) circle. Drizzle the remaining olive oil over the top and scatter with the zucchini, fior di latte and remaining garlic.

Carefully transfer the pizza to the hot pizza stone and bake for 8–10 minutes, until the crust is golden and cooked through, and the cheese is melted.

Top the pizza with the stracciatella and a little shaved pecorino. Add the zucchini petals, herbs and a drizzle of olive oil, and serve with lemon wedges on the side, if desired.

SMOKED BUFFALO MOZZARELLA, LEMON & ARTICHOKE

 Makes 1 × 24 cm (9½ in) pizza

1 × 220 g (8 oz) Neapolitan pizza dough ball (page 14)

1 teaspoon extra virgin olive oil, plus extra for drizzling

80 g (2¾ oz) smoked buffalo mozzarella, torn

6 very thin slices lemon, seeds removed

3–4 thyme sprigs, leaves picked, plus extra to garnish (optional)

6 thin wedges marinated artichoke hearts

basil leaves, to serve (optional)

Place a pizza stone on the bottom rack of the cold oven. Set the oven to its highest temperature (ideally 260°C/500°F fan-forced) and preheat for 1 hour.

Following the instructions on page 14, use your hands to press, pat and stretch the dough ball out to form a 24 cm (9½ in) circle. Lightly brush the dough with the olive oil, then top with half the mozzarella and all of the lemon, thyme and artichoke. Add the remaining cheese, then season with salt and pepper.

Carefully transfer the pizza to the hot pizza stone and bake for 8–10 minutes, until the crust is golden and cooked through, and the cheese is melted and bubbling.

Drizzle the pizza with a little olive oil and scatter with basil or thyme leaves, if desired.

SMOKED MUSSEL

 Makes 1 × 24 cm (9½ in) pizza

80 g (2¾ oz) smoked mussels in oil, drained

1 garlic clove, very finely chopped

2 anchovy fillets in oil, finely chopped

1–1½ teaspoons baby capers, rinsed and drained

good pinch of chilli flakes

2 teaspoons chopped parsley, plus extra to serve

½ teaspoon lemon zest

1 × 220 g (8 oz) Neapolitan pizza dough ball (page 14)

1 teaspoon extra virgin olive oil, plus extra for drizzling

65 g (2¼ oz) fior di latte, torn

small handful of freshly grated Grana Pandano

chopped basil leaves, to serve (optional)

chilli oil, for drizzling (optional)

Place a pizza stone on the bottom rack of the cold oven. Set the oven to its highest temperature (ideally 260°C/500°F fan-forced) and preheat for 1 hour.

Combine the mussels, garlic, anchovy fillets, capers, chilli flakes, parsley and lemon zest in a bowl, season with salt and pepper and set aside.

Following the instructions on page 14, use your hands to press, pat and stretch the dough ball out to form a 24 cm (9½ in) circle. Drizzle the olive oil over the dough and lightly brush to cover it. Top with the fior di latte, prepared mussels and Grana Pandano, and drizzle with a little olive oil.

Carefully transfer the pizza to the hot pizza stone and bake for 8–10 minutes, until the crust is golden and cooked through, and the cheese is melted.

Finish the cooked pizza with an extra scattering of parsley and, if desired, basil and a small drizzle of chilli oil.

PUMPKIN *with* GOAT'S CHEESE & TOASTED PINE NUTS

 Makes 1 × 24 cm (9½ in) pizza

150 g (5½ oz) butternut pumpkin (squash), peeled and diced into 2 cm (¾ in) pieces

1 teaspoon extra virgin olive oil

1 × 220 g (8 oz) Neapolitan pizza dough ball (page 14)

60 g (¼ cup) San Marzano tomato sauce (page 22)

60 g (2 oz) buffalo mozzarella, torn

4–6 sage leaves

25 g (1 oz) goat's cheese

small handful of rocket (arugula)

1 teaspoon pine nuts, toasted

extra virgin olive oil, for drizzling

OLIVE TAPENADE

130 g (1 cup) kalamata olives, pitted

80 ml (⅓ cup) extra virgin olive oil

2–3 anchovy fillets in oil

5–6 basil leaves

1 garlic clove

1 tablespoon capers, rinsed and drained

1 teaspoon sherry vinegar

¼ teaspoon chilli flakes

freshly ground black pepper

large handful of parsley leaves, finely chopped

Place a pizza stone on the bottom rack of the cold oven and preheat the oven to 200°C (400°F) fan-forced.

To make the olive tapenade (see Notes), place all the ingredients except the parsley in the small bowl of a food processor and pulse until combined. Transfer the mixture to a bowl, add the parsley and stir through. Taste and season with a little more chilli or a pinch of salt, if desired.

On a baking tray, toss the pumpkin in the olive oil and season with salt and pepper. Roast in the oven for 6 minutes, then turn the pumpkin over and roast for a further 6–8 minutes, until cooked through. Set aside to cool slightly.

Increase the oven to its highest temperature (ideally 260°C/500°F fan-forced) and preheat for 45 minutes.

Meanwhile, prepare the dough. Following the instructions on page 14, use your hands to press, pat and stretch the dough ball out to form a 24 cm (9½ in) circle. Spread the San Marzano tomato sauce over the dough and top with the mozzarella, sage and roasted pumpkin.

Carefully transfer the pizza to the hot pizza stone and bake for 8–10 minutes, until the crust is golden and cooked through, and the cheese is melted and bubbling.

Crumble the goat's cheese over the cooked pizza and top with the rocket and toasted pine nuts. To serve, finish with a little olive oil, pepper and a drizzle of olive tapenade.

Notes: To make this pizza vegetarian, swap out the tapenade with the Basil pesto or Lemony kale pesto (page 25).

This tapenade recipe will make about 170 g (⅔ cup). Left-over tapenade will keep in an airtight container in the fridge for 5–7 days.

THE BREAKFAST

NEW CLASSICS

Makes 1 × 24 cm (9½ in) pizza

2 pieces (65 g/2¼ oz) short-cut bacon, sliced into 3 cm (1 in) strips

30 g (⅔ cup) baby spinach leaves

1 × 220 g (8 oz) Neapolitan pizza dough ball (page 14)

1 teaspoon extra virgin olive oil

50 g (1¾ oz) fior di latte, torn

handful of gruyere, grated

1 egg

freshly grated Grana Padano, to serve

Place a pizza stone on the bottom rack of the cold oven. Set the oven to its highest temperature (ideally 260°C/500°F fan-forced) and preheat for 1 hour.

Place a non-stick frying pan over medium heat. Add the bacon and fry for about 2 minutes, until lightly rendered, then remove from the pan and drain on paper towels. Add the spinach to the pan and wilt in the bacon fat for just a minute, then remove from the heat and set aside.

Following the instructions on page 14, use your hands to press, pat and stretch the dough ball out to form a 24 cm (9½ in) circle. Lightly brush the olive oil over the dough and top with the fior di latte. Evenly distribute the bacon and spinach over the base, top with the gruyere, then crack the egg into the centre of the pizza.

Carefully transfer the pizza to the hot pizza stone and bake for 8–10 minutes, until the crust is golden and cooked through, the cheese is melted and bubbling, and the egg is cooked through.

Top with the Grana Padano, season with salt and pepper and enjoy!

THE HAWAIIAN

 Makes 1 × 24 cm (9½ in) pizza

1 piece (40 g/1½ oz) bacon, sliced into 3 cm (1¼ in) pieces

1 × 220 g (8 oz) Neapolitan pizza dough ball (page 14)

60 g (¼ cup) San Marzano tomato sauce (page 22)

110 g (¾ cup) shredded low-moisture mozzarella

2 slices ham (45 g/1½ oz), torn

50 g (¼ cup) diced tinned pineapple, well drained

10 slices pickled jalapenos, to serve (optional)

1 tablespoon hot honey, to serve (optional; see Note)

Note: Hot honey is chilli-infused honey, which lends a spicy-sweet kick to pizza. It can be purchased at delicatessens and some supermarkets.

Place a pizza stone on the bottom rack of the cold oven. Set the oven to its highest temperature (ideally 260°C/500°F fan-forced) and preheat for 1 hour.

Place a non-stick frying pan over medium–low heat, add the bacon and fry for 1½–2 minutes, until lightly rendered. Remove from the pan and drain on paper towels.

Following the instructions on page 14, use your hands to press, pat and stretch the dough ball out to form a 24 cm (9½ in) circle. Spread the San Marzano tomato sauce over the dough, sprinkle over the mozzarella and top with the bacon, ham and pineapple.

Carefully transfer the pizza to the hot pizza stone and bake for 8–10 minutes, until the crust is golden and cooked through, and the cheese is melted and bubbling.

For a spicy twist, add the jalapenos and hot honey.

WAGYU BRESAOLA

 Makes 1 × 24 cm (9½ in) pizza

1 × 220 g (8 oz) Neapolitan pizza dough ball (page 14)

80 g (⅓ cup) San Marzano tomato sauce (page 22)

65 g (2¼ oz) buffalo mozzarella, torn

handful of rocket (arugula)

½ teaspoon aged balsamic vinegar

1 teaspoon extra virgin olive oil

6 slices wagyu bresaola

shaved parmesan, to serve

Place a pizza stone on the bottom rack of the cold oven. Set the oven to its highest temperature (ideally 260°C/500°F fan-forced) and preheat for 1 hour.

Following the instructions on page 14, use your hands to press, pat and stretch the dough ball out to form a 24 cm (9½ in) circle. Spoon the San Marzano tomato sauce over the dough and top with the mozzarella.

Carefully transfer the pizza to the hot pizza stone and bake for 8–10 minutes, until the crust is golden and cooked through, and the cheese is melted and bubbling.

Meanwhile, toss the rocket, balsamic vinegar and olive oil in a small bowl. Season with salt and pepper, to taste.

Top the cooked pizza with the wagyu bresaola, and scatter with the prepared rocket and shaved parmesan.

PEACH & GOAT'S CHEESE *with* CANDIED WALNUTS & BALSAMIC GLAZE

 Makes 1 × 24 cm (9½ in) pizza

1 peach, cut into 8 wedges

1 teaspoon honey

1 × 220 g (8 oz) Neapolitan pizza dough ball (page 14)

1 teaspoon extra virgin olive oil

60 g (2 oz) fior di latte, torn

45 g (1½ oz) ashed goat's cheese, crumbled

freshly grated Grana Pandano, to serve

2–3 small radicchio leaves, torn

1½ teaspoons balsamic glaze (see Note)

2 teaspoons candied walnuts, roughly chopped

Note: Balsamic glaze is a thick balsamic reduction available at most supermarkets.

Place a pizza stone on the bottom rack of the cold oven. Set the oven to its highest temperature (ideally 260°C/500°F fan-forced) and preheat for 1 hour.

In a small bowl, toss the peach wedges in the honey. Heat a non-stick chargrill pan over medium–high heat, and chargrill the peach for 1 minute each side, until lightly charred and softened. Remove from the pan and set aside.

Following the instructions on page 14, use your hands to press, pat and stretch the dough ball out to form a 24 cm (9½ in) circle. Lightly brush the olive oil over the dough and top with the charred peach, fior di latte and goat's cheese.

Carefully transfer the pizza to the hot pizza stone and bake for 8–10 minutes, until the crust is golden and cooked through, and the cheese is melted.

Scatter the Grana Pandano over the cooked pizza and season with salt and pepper. Top with the radicchio leaves, drizzle with the balsamic glaze and finish with the candied walnuts.

BBQ CHICKEN

 Makes 1 × 24 cm (9½ in) pizza

1 × 220 g (8 oz) Neapolitan pizza dough ball (page 14)

60 g (⅓ cup) shredded roast chicken

125 ml (½ cup) barbecue sauce of your choice

40 g (1½ oz) smoked mozzarella, shredded

40 g (1½ oz) gouda, shredded

15 g (½ oz) small red onion, sliced

8 slices pickled jalapenos

1–2 tablespoons ranch dressing

Place a pizza stone on the bottom rack of the cold oven. Set the oven to its highest temperature (ideally 260°C/500°F fan-forced) and preheat for 1 hour.

Following the instructions on page 14, use your hands to press, pat and stretch the dough ball out to form a 24 cm (9½ in) circle.

Mix the chicken and 60 ml (¼ cup) of the barbecue sauce together. Spread the remaining barbecue sauce over the dough and top with half the mozzarella, half the gouda, and all of the chicken. Scatter over the red onion, jalapeno and remaining cheese.

Carefully transfer the pizza to the hot pizza stone and bake for 8–10 minutes, until the crust is golden and cooked through, and the cheese is melted and bubbling.

Remove from the oven, drizzle with the ranch dressing and serve.

SPICY LAMB

 Makes 1 × 24 cm (9½ in) pizza

60 g (¼ cup) San Marzano tomato sauce (page 22)

1–2 teaspoons harissa paste, to taste

¼ teaspoon ground cumin

⅛ teaspoon ground cinnamon

good pinch of Aleppo pepper

1 × 220 g (8 oz) Neapolitan pizza dough ball (page 14)

100 g (3½ oz) Merguez lamb sausage (see Notes), casings removed, crumbled into small pieces (about 5 g/¼ oz)

15 g (½ oz) small red onion, sliced

50 g (1¾ oz) feta, crumbled

8–10 mint leaves

2 teaspoons toasted pine nuts

lemon wedges, to serve

LEMONY TAHINI YOGHURT SAUCE

250 g (1 cup) Greek yoghurt

3 tablespoons hulled tahini

1 tablespoon lemon juice, plus 1 teaspoon zest

sea salt, to taste

Place a pizza stone on the bottom rack of the cold oven. Set the oven to its highest temperature (ideally 260°C/500°F fan-forced) and preheat for 1 hour.

To make the lemony tahini yoghurt sauce, place all the ingredients in a bowl and whisk to combine. Add a little water for a thinner sauce, if desired. Transfer to an airtight container and refrigerate (see Notes).

In a small bowl, combine the San Marzano tomato sauce with the harissa paste, cumin, cinnamon, Aleppo pepper and a good pinch of salt. Set aside.

Following the instructions on page 14, use your hands to press, pat and stretch the dough ball out to form a 24 cm (9½ in) circle. Spoon the prepared tomato sauce over the dough, then top with the sausage. (Make sure that the pieces of sausage are small, or they won't cook through during the baking time.) Scatter with the red onion and feta.

Carefully transfer the pizza to the hot pizza stone and bake for 8–10 minutes, until the crust is golden and cooked through, and the cheese is melted.

Scatter the mint leaves and pine nuts over the pizza and finish with a drizzle of the lemony tahini yoghurt sauce. Serve with lemon wedges on the side.

Notes: Merguez sausages are hot, spiced lamb sausages from North Africa, flavoured with spices such as cayenne pepper, hot paprika and fennel. They can be purchased at international delicatessens and gourmet butchers.

The recipe for the yoghurt sauce makes about 315 ml (1¼ cups). Left-over sauce will keep in the fridge for 5–6 days.

KIMCHI & SESAME

 Makes 1 × 24 cm (9½ in) pizza

80 g (⅓ cup) San Marzano tomato sauce (page 22)

¾ teaspoon gochujang (see Notes)

1 × 220 g (8 oz) Neapolitan pizza dough ball (page 14)

80 g (2¾ oz) fior di latte, torn

50 g (¼ cup) drained and chopped kimchi

toasted sesame seeds, to serve

thinly sliced spring onion (scallion), to serve

1–2 drops of toasted sesame oil (see Notes)

sriracha mayonnaise, to serve

Notes: Gochujang is a spicy-sweet fermented chilli paste, available in most supermarkets.

Toasted sesame oil is potent stuff – just a few drops are required.

Place a pizza stone on the bottom rack of the cold oven. Set the oven to its highest temperature (ideally 260°C/500°F fan-forced) and preheat for 1 hour.

Place the San Marzano pizza sauce and gochujang in a small bowl and stir to combine.

Following the instructions on page 14, use your hands to press, pat and stretch the dough ball out to form a 24 cm (9½ in) circle. Spoon the prepared tomato sauce over the dough and top with half the fior di latte. Finish with the kimchi, followed by the remaining cheese.

Carefully transfer the pizza to the hot pizza stone and bake for 8–10 minutes, until the crust is golden and cooked through, and the cheese is melted.

Sprinkle the toasted sesame seeds, a few slices of spring onion and the toasted sesame oil (see Notes) over the pizza. Drizzle with a little sriracha mayonnaise in a zig-zag motion and enjoy!

ĆEVAPČIĆI & AJVAR

NEW CLASSICS

 Makes 1 × 24 cm (9½ in) pizza

1 × 220 g (8 oz) Neapolitan pizza dough ball (page 14)

60 g (¼ cup) ajvar (see Notes)

20 g (¾ oz) provolone, shredded

50 g (⅓ cup) sliced low-moisture mozzarella

120 g (4½ oz) ćevapčići meat (see Notes)

¼ small red onion, thinly sliced

25 g (1 oz) sheep's feta, crumbled

1 tablespoon chopped parsley leaves

Garlic oil (page 24), for drizzling

pepperoncini (see Notes), to serve

Notes: Ajvar is a Croatian roasted red bell pepper (capsicum) and eggplant (aubergine) condiment.

Ćevapčići is a skinless Croatian sausage, usually made from a mix of beef, pork and lamb.

Pepperoncini are pickled chillies.

You can find all these ingredients at international delicatessens and some supermarkets.

Place a pizza stone on the bottom rack of the cold oven. Set the oven to its highest temperature (ideally 260°C/500°F fan-forced) and preheat for 1 hour.

Following the instructions on page 14, use your hands to press, pat and stretch the dough ball out to form a 24 cm (9½ in) circle. Spoon the ajvar over the dough, then top with the provolone and half the mozzarella.

Tear the ćevapčići into small pieces (about 5 g/¼ oz) and place on top of the cheese. (It's important to ensure that the pieces are small or they won't cook through during the baking time.) Scatter over the red onion, feta and remaining mozzarella.

Carefully transfer the pizza to the hot pizza stone and bake for 8–10 minutes, until the crust is golden and cooked through, and the cheese is melted.

Scatter the parsley over the pizza, drizzle with garlic oil and season with salt and pepper, to taste. Serve with pepperoncini on the side.

SPICY MEXICAN SWEETCORN *with* SMOKED MOZZARELLA

 Makes 1 × 24 cm (9½ in) pizza

60 ml (¼ cup) San Marzano tomato sauce (page 22)

4 teaspoons chipotle in adobo sauce

1 × 220 g (8 oz) Neapolitan pizza dough ball (page 14)

50 g (⅓ cup) smoked mozzarella, grated or shredded

20 g (¾ oz) queso fresco or feta

50 g (¼ cup) sweetcorn kernels

8 pickled jalapenos slices

2–3 teaspoons shaved parmesan

¼ avocado, sliced (optional)

8 coriander (cilantro) leaves

1½ tablespoons crema (see Notes)

lime wedges, to serve

PICKLED RED ONION

125 g (4½ oz) red onion, thinly sliced

1 garlic clove, thinly sliced

1 red bird's eye chilli, split

2 allspice berries

1 bay leaf

¼ teaspoon black peppercorns

125 ml (½ cup) apple cider vinegar

60 ml (¼ cup) lime juice

2 tablespoons caster (superfine) sugar

1 teaspoon sea salt

To make the pickled red onion, place the onion in a heatproof bowl, cover with boiling water and leave for 20–30 seconds. Drain and refresh under cold running water. Transfer the onion to a large glass jar, add the remaining ingredients, cover, seal and allow to pickle for at least 45–60 minutes (see Notes).

Place a pizza stone on the bottom rack of the cold oven. Set the oven to its highest temperature (ideally 260°C/500°F fan-forced) and preheat for 1 hour.

Place the San Marzano tomato sauce and the chipotle in a small bowl and stir to combine.

Following the instructions on page 14, use your hands to press, pat and stretch the dough ball out to form a 24 cm (9½ in) circle. Spoon the prepared tomato sauce over the dough and top with the mozzarella, queso fresco or feta, sweetcorn, jalapeno and a few slices of pickled red onion.

Carefully transfer the pizza to the hot pizza stone and bake for 8–10 minutes, until the crust is golden and cooked through, and the cheese is melted.

Scatter the parmesan, avocado (if using) and a few coriander leaves over the top of the pizza. Finish with a good zig-zag of crema, and serve with lime wedges on the side.

Notes: If you can't find crema, you can use sour cream instead.

The onion is ready after 45–60 minutes, but the flavour will intensify the longer the onion is stored in the fridge.

This pickled onion recipe makes about 325 g (1½ cups). Left-over onion will keep in an airtight container in the fridge for about 2 weeks.

PEA PESTO, SPINACH & PISTACHIO

 Makes 1 × 24 cm (9½ in) pizza

1 × 220 g (8 oz) Neapolitan pizza dough ball (page 14)

1 teaspoon extra virgin olive oil

70 g (2½ oz) fior di latte, torn

small handful of baby spinach leaves and pea tendrils, to serve

1½ teaspoons finely snipped chives

1 tablespoon slivered pistachios

1–1½ tablespoons freshly grated Grana Pandano

lemon wedges, to serve

BASIL OIL

50 g (1½ cups) packed basil leaves

125 ml (½ cup) extra virgin olive oil

PEA PESTO

260 g (2 cups) frozen peas, thawed

large handful of basil leaves

2 garlic cloves, peeled

55 g (2 oz) freshly grated Grana Pandano

60 ml (¼ cup) extra virgin olive oil

zest and juice of 1 lemon (about 3 tablespoons juice)

sea salt and freshly ground black pepper, to taste

Place a pizza stone on the bottom rack of the cold oven. Set the oven to its highest temperature (ideally 260°C/500°F fan-forced) and preheat for 1 hour.

To make the basil oil, blanch the basil leaves in boiling water for about 8 seconds, then plunge into iced water. Drain and squeeze the water out of the basil, then transfer to a blender. Add the olive oil and a pinch of salt and blitz for about 20–30 seconds, until well pureed. Allow the oil to settle for 20–30 minutes, then strain through a piece of fine muslin (cheesecloth) into a jar. Discard the solids (see Notes).

To make the pea pesto, place all the ingredients in a food processor and blitz until smooth and well combined (see Notes).

Following the instructions on page 14, use your hands to press, pat and stretch the dough ball out to form a 24 cm (9½ in) circle. Lightly brush half the olive oil over the dough and spread 90 g (⅓ cup) of the pea pesto over the top. Scatter with the fior di latte and drizzle over the remaining olive oil.

Carefully transfer the pizza to the hot pizza stone and bake for 8–10 minutes, until the crust is golden and cooked through, and the cheese is melted and bubbling.

Top the pizza with the spinach, pea tendrils, chives, pistachios and Grana Pandano, drizzle with basil oil and season with pepper. Serve with lemon wedges on the side.

Notes: This basil oil recipe makes about 125 ml (½ cup). Left-over oil will keep in an airtight container in the fridge for 5–7 days – bring to room temperature before using.

Like the basil oil, you'll have more pesto than you need for a single pizza – this recipe makes about 375 g (1½ cups). Transfer any left-over pesto to an airtight container and store in the fridge for up to 5 days.

POTATO, ROSEMARY & TRUFFLE OIL FOCACCIA

Makes 1 × 23 × 33 cm (9 × 13 in) focaccia

140 g (5 oz) all-purpose potato, thinly sliced (preferably using a mandoline; see Note)

1½ tablespoons truffle-infused olive oil

½ teaspoon freshly ground black pepper

1 × prepared Focaccia dough (see page 16)

1 tablespoon rosemary leaves

1 tablespoon extra virgin olive oil

sea salt flakes

Note: For an even easier focaccia, skip the potatoes and simply drizzle your dimpled dough with olive oil. Sprinkle over salt flakes and rosemary or oregano. Bake as instructed in the main recipe.

Preheat the oven to 200°C (400°F) fan-forced, and place a rack on the middle shelf in the oven.

Toss the potato with the truffle-infused olive oil and pepper in a bowl, and set aside for 15 minutes to infuse.

Meanwhile, press lightly oiled fingers into the dough to create dimples up and down the entire surface. Scatter over the marinated slices of potato and rosemary, ensuring even coverage. Use your fingers to lightly press the potato and rosemary into the dough, then top with the extra virgin olive oil and a little salt.

Carefully transfer the focaccia to the middle rack of the oven and bake for about 20 minutes, until golden and cooked through.

Place the pan on a wire rack and allow to cool just slightly before transferring the focaccia to a chopping board. Delicious served hot, warm or at room temperature.

RICOTTA & PESTO FOCACCIA

Makes 1 × 23 × 33 cm (9 × 13 in) focaccia

1 × prepared Focaccia dough (see page 16)

250 g (1 cup) San Marzano tomato sauce (page 22)

20 g (¾ oz) freshly grated parmesan

400 g (2 cups) buffalo ricotta

80–125 g (⅓–½ cup) Basil pesto (page 25)

extra virgin olive oil, for drizzling

24 basil leaves

Preheat the oven to 200°C (400°F) fan-forced, and place a rack on the middle shelf in the oven.

Press lightly oiled fingers into the dough to create dimples up and down the entire surface.

Carefully transfer the dough to the middle rack of the oven and bake for about 20 minutes, until golden and cooked through.

Remove the pan from the oven and spread the San Marzano tomato sauce over the focaccia, then bake for another 8 minutes.

Place the pan on a wire rack and immediately sprinkle the parmesan over the focaccia. Allow to cool just slightly before transferring the focaccia to a chopping board.

Cut into eight slices and top each with 50 g (1¾ oz) of the ricotta. Dollop over a little (or a lot) of the pesto and drizzle with a little olive oil. Finish with three basil leaves on each slice and enjoy!

PISSALADIÈRE

 Makes 1 23 × 33 cm (9 × 13 in) pissaladière

720 g (3 cups) Caramelised onions (page 24)

1 × prepared Detroit-style pizza dough (page 20)

180 g (6½ oz) anchovy fillets in oil

24 black niçoise olives, pitted (optional; see Note)

Note: Omit the olives for an Italian-style pissaladiera.

Preheat the oven to 220°C (430°F) fan-forced, and place a rack on the middle shelf in the oven.

Evenly spread the caramelised onions over the dough, then use the anchovies to make a lattice or diamond pattern over the onion. If using the olives, place one in the centre of each diamond.

Carefully transfer the pissaladière to the middle rack of the oven and bake for 12–15 minutes, until golden and cooked through.

Place the pan on a wire rack and let the pissaladière cool for 5–10 minutes.

Carefully transfer the pissaladière to a chopping board and cut into eight to ten slices to serve.

DETROIT-STYLE HOTTIE

DEEP PAN

Makes 1 × 25.5 × 35.5 cm (10 × 14 in) pizza

1 teaspoon olive oil

100 g (3½ oz) spicy Italian pork sausage, casings removed

1 × prepared Detroit-style pizza dough (page 20)

350 g (12½ oz) Wisconsin brick cheese or low-moisture mozzarella, diced into 1.5 cm (½ in) cubes

50 g (1¾ oz) chilli-coated salami, sliced

50 g (1¾ oz) smoked ham, diced into 1.5 cm (½ in) cubes

250–375 g (1–1½ cups) Marinara sauce (page 22)

chilli flakes, to serve

Preheat the oven to its highest temperature (ideally 260°C/500°F fan-forced), and place a rack on the lowest shelf in the oven.

Add the olive oil to a frying pan over medium heat and crumble in the sausage. Cook for 2–3 minutes, until lightly browned, then drain the excess oil and set the sausage aside to cool.

Top the dough with the cheese, making sure that it reaches the sides of the pizza; this will ensure edges of crisp, melted cheese – a signature trait of Detroit-style pizza.

Scatter the sausage, salami and ham over the dough, then spoon over the marinara sauce in two long strips, or 'racing stripes'.

Carefully transfer the pizza to the bottom rack of the oven and bake for 12–15 minutes, until the crust is golden and cooked through, and the cheese is melted and bubbling.

Place the pan on a wire rack and immediately run a butter knife around the edges of the crust to loosen the melted cheese and avoid it sticking. Let the pizza cool for a few minutes, then carefully transfer to a large chopping board.

Sprinkle the pizza with a few good pinches of chilli flakes, as desired, then cut into slices and serve.

DETROIT-STYLE PEPPERONI

DEEP PAN

Makes 1 × 25.5 × 35.5 cm (10 × 14 in) pizza

1 × prepared Detroit-style pizza dough (page 20)

150 g (5½ oz) pepperoni, cut into 3 mm (⅛ in) thick slices

350 g (12½ oz) Wisconsin brick cheese, low-moisture mozzarella or an equal mixture of cheddar and low-moisture mozzarella, diced into 1.5 cm (½ in) cubes

375 g (1½ cups) Marinara sauce (page 22)

finely grated parmesan, to serve

salt flakes, to serve (optional)

Preheat the oven to its highest temperature (ideally 260°C/500°F fan-forced), and place a rack on the lowest shelf in the oven.

Layer the dough with half the pepperoni and all the cheese, making sure that it reaches the sides of the pizza. This will ensure edges of crisp, melted cheese – a signature trait of Detroit-style pizza.

Add the remaining pepperoni and spoon over the marinara sauce in two long strips, or 'racing stripes'.

Carefully transfer the pizza to the bottom rack of the oven and bake for 12–15 minutes, until the crust is golden and cooked through, and the cheese is melted and bubbling.

Place the pan on a wire rack and immediately run a butter knife around the edges of the crust to loosen the melted cheese and avoid it sticking.

Let the pizza cool for a few minutes, then carefully transfer to a large chopping board. Season with parmesan and salt flakes, if desired. Cut into slices and enjoy!

DETROIT-STYLE ULTIMATE ANTIPASTO

 Makes 1 × 25.5 × 35.5 cm (10 × 14 in) pizza

1 × prepared Detroit-style pizza dough (page 20)

300 g (10½ oz) Wisconsin brick cheese or low-moisture mozzarella, diced into 1.5 cm (½ in) cubes

50 g (1¾ oz) red onion, sliced

50 g (1¾ oz) marinated bell pepper (capsicum), drained and sliced

50 g (1¾ oz) marinated grilled eggplant (aubergine), sliced

50 g (1¾ oz) marinated artichoke hearts, sliced

250 g (1 cup) Marinara sauce (see page 22)

chilli flakes, for sprinkling

basil leaves, to serve

Preheat the oven to its highest temperature (ideally 260°C/500°F fan-forced), and place a rack on the lowest shelf in the oven.

Top the dough with the cheese, making sure that it reaches the sides of the pizza; this will ensure edges of crisp, melted cheese – a signature trait of Detroit-style pizza.

Top the dough with the onion, bell pepper, eggplant and artichoke, then spoon over the marinara sauce in three long strips, or 'racing stripes'.

Carefully transfer the pizza to the bottom rack of the oven and bake for 12–15 minutes, until the crust is golden and cooked through, and the cheese is melted and bubbling.

Place the pan on a wire rack and immediately run a butter knife around the edges of the crust to loosen the melted cheese and avoid it sticking. Let the pizza cool for a few minutes, then carefully transfer to a large chopping board.

Sprinkle the pizza with a good pinch of chilli flakes and finish with a few basil leaves.

GRANDMA-STYLE MORTADELLA, BURRATA & PISTACHIO

DEEP PAN

 Makes 1 × 25 × 38 cm (10 × 15 in) pizza

1 × Detroit-style pizza dough, prepared grandma-style (see page 20)

2½ teaspoons extra virgin olive oil, plus extra for drizzling

1 teaspoon chopped rosemary leaves

good pinch of sea salt flakes, plus extra to serve

5 × 120 g (4½ oz) burrata balls, torn in half

10 thin slices mortadella

2 tablespoons chopped pistachio kernels

20 basil leaves

Preheat the oven to 220°C (430°F) fan-forced, and place a rack on the middle shelf in the oven.

Drizzle the dough with the olive oil and sprinkle with the rosemary and sea salt flakes.

Carefully transfer the dough to the middle rack of the oven and bake for 12–15 minutes, until the crust is golden and lightly crisped.

Place the pan on a wire rack and immediately run a butter knife around the edges of the crust to loosen it. Let the pizza cool for a few minutes before carefully transferring to a large chopping board.

Cut the pizza into ten slices, and top each with half a burrata ball, spreading over the burrata's creamy centre. Add a slice of the mortadella and a sprinkle of the pistachio kernels, then finish with the basil leaves, a little dusting of salt and pepper and a drizzle of extra virgin olive oil.

GRANDMA-STYLE SWEET & SPICY

DEEP PAN

Makes 1 × 25 × 38 cm (10 × 15 in) pizza

1 × Detroit-style pizza dough, prepared grandma-style (see page 20)

6 anchovy fillets in oil, chopped

1 tablespoon pickled jalapenos, chopped

1 teaspoon dried oregano

1 teaspoon chilli flakes, plus extra to serve

300 g (3 cups) shredded low-moisture mozzarella

80 g (2¾ oz) spicy salami of your choice, sliced

185 g (¾ cup) San Marzano tomato sauce (page 22)

2 tablespoons hot honey (see Note)

Note: Hot honey is chilli-infused honey, which lends a spicy-sweet kick to pizza. It can be purchased at delicatessens and some supermarkets.

Preheat the oven to 220°C (430°F) fan-forced, and place a rack on the middle shelf in the oven.

Top the dough with the anchovy fillets, jalapeno, oregano and chilli flakes. Add the mozzarella and spicy salami, then drizzle with the San Marzano tomato sauce, leaving some cheese and salami exposed.

Carefully transfer the pizza to the middle rack of the oven and bake for 12–15 minutes, until the crust is golden and lightly crisped, and the cheese is melted and bubbling.

Place the pan on a wire rack and immediately run a butter knife around the edges of the crust to loosen it, then drizzle the honey over the pizza. Allow to cool for a few minutes, then carefully transfer the pizza to a large chopping board.

Cut the pizza into ten slices and serve with extra chilli flakes on the side.

CHICAGO-STYLE SAUSAGE PIE

 Makes 1 × 26.5 cm (10½ in) pizza

plain (all-purpose) flour, for
dusting

1 × Chicago-style pizza dough ball
(page 19)

400 g (14 oz) low-moisture
mozzarella, sliced

500 g (1 lb 2 oz) Italian sausage,
casings removed, crumbled into
small pieces

625–750 g (2½– 3 cups) Marinara
sauce (page 22; see Note)

55 g (½ cup) finely grated
parmesan, plus extra to serve

1 teaspoon olive oil

FOR THE CAST-IRON FRYING PAN

2 teaspoons butter

2 tablespoons olive oil

2 tablespoons freshly grated
parmesan (optional)

Note: You want to ensure that the
marinara sauce is cooked down and thick,
not wet and runny, or your pie will be
soupy and sloppy.

Preheat the oven to 220°C (430°F) fan-forced, and place a rack on the lowest shelf in the oven.

Grease a 26.5 cm (10½ in) cast-iron frying pan with the butter and olive oil, then sprinkle with the parmesan (if using).

On a floured surface, roll the dough out to form a 35.5 cm (14 in) circle. Transfer the dough to the prepared pan, then press the dough evenly into the pan's base and side. Cover and set aside for 5–10 minutes to rest.

Evenly scatter the mozzarella over the dough, covering the entire surface. Top with the sausage, marinara sauce and parmesan, then brush the edge of the crust with the olive oil.

Carefully transfer the pizza to the lowest rack in the oven and bake for 30–40 minutes, until the crust is golden and cooked through, and the cheese is melted.

Sprinkle a little more parmesan over the pizza, if desired. Rest the pizza for 12–15 minutes in the pan, then carefully transfer to a chopping board, cut into slices and serve.

CHICAGO-STYLE VEGGIE PIE

Makes 1 × 26.5 cm (10½ in) pizza

plain (all-purpose) flour, for dusting

1 × Chicago-style pizza dough ball (page 19)

300 g (10½ oz) low-moisture mozzarella, thinly sliced

100 g (3½ oz) provolone, thinly sliced

200 g (7 oz) Caramelised onions (page 24)

100 g (3½ oz) roasted bell pepper (capsicum), drained and sliced

50 g (1¾ oz) black olives, sliced

625–750 g (2½–3 cups) Marinara sauce (page 22; see Note)

50 g (½ cup) finely grated parmesan, plus extra to serve (optional)

1 teaspoon olive oil

FOR THE CAST-IRON FRYING PAN

2 teaspoons butter

2 tablespoons olive oil

Note: You want to ensure that the marinara sauce is cooked down and thick, not wet and runny, or your pie will be soupy and sloppy.

Preheat the oven to 220°C (430°F) fan-forced, and place a rack on the lowest shelf in the oven.

Grease a 26.5 cm (10½ in) cast-iron frying pan with the butter and olive oil.

On a floured surface, roll the dough out to a 35.5 cm (14 in) circle. Transfer the dough to the prepared pan, then press the dough evenly into the pan's base and side. Cover and set aside for 5–10 minutes to rest.

Evenly scatter the mozzarella and provolone over the dough, covering the entire surface. Top with the caramelised onions, bell pepper and olives, add the marinara sauce and parmesan, and brush the edge of the crust with the olive oil.

Carefully transfer the pizza to the lowest rack in the oven and bake for 30–40 minutes, until the crust is golden and cooked through, and the cheese is melted and bubbling.

Sprinkle a little more parmesan over the pizza, if desired. Rest the pizza for 12–15 minutes in the pan, then carefully transfer to a chopping board, cut into slices and serve.

SOPRESSA & OLIVE PANZEROTTI

 Makes 10 panzerotti

plain (all-purpose) flour, for dusting

10 × 80 g (2¾ oz) Fried & sweet dough balls (page 21)

150 g (5½ oz) Marinara sauce (page 22)

300 g (10½ oz) fresh mozzarella, sliced or torn

20 slices sopressa, diced

30 g (¼ cup) sliced black olives

2 teaspoons oregano leaves

1 litre (1 quart) vegetable oil, for deep-frying

salt flakes, to serve

On a lightly floured surface, flatten a dough ball and roll it out to a 16 cm (6¼ in) circle. Spoon 1 tablespoon of the marinara sauce over the centre and add 30 g (1 oz) of the mozzarella, about 2 teaspoons of the sopressa and a few slices of olive. Season with the oregano and salt.

Lightly brush the edge of the dough with a little water. Fold the panzerotti in half and firmly press the edges together, then fold the edge over and crimp to seal. Repeat with the remaining ingredients to make ten panzerotti.

In a large saucepan, heat the oil over medium–high heat to 175°C–180°C (345°F–350°F) on a kitchen thermometer.

Carefully fry two to three panzerotti at a time, depending on the size of your pan. Fry for about 2 minutes, until puffed, crisp and golden. Remove with a slotted spoon and drain on paper towels.

Season the panzerotti with salt flakes and serve immediately.

MOZZARELLA & ANCHOVY PANZEROTTI

FRIED AND STUFFED

 Makes 10 panzerotti

plain (all-purpose) flour, for dusting

10 × 80 g (2¾ oz) Fried & sweet dough balls (page 21)

150 g (5½ oz) Marinara sauce (see page 22)

300 g (10 ½ oz) fresh mozzarella, sliced or torn

10 white anchovy fillets in oil, drained

10 basil leaves

1 litre (1 quart) vegetable oil, for deep-frying

salt flakes, to serve

On a lightly floured surface, flatten a dough ball and roll it out to a 16 cm (6¼ in) circle. Spoon 1 tablespoon of marinara sauce over the centre and add 30 g (1 oz) of the mozzarella, one anchovy fillet and one basil leaf.

Lightly brush the edge of the dough with a little water. Fold the panzerotti in half and firmly press the edges together, then fold the edge over and crimp to seal. Repeat with the remaining ingredients to make ten panzerotti.

In a large saucepan, heat the oil over medium–high heat to 175°C–180°C (345°F–350°F) on a kitchen thermometer.

Carefully fry two to three panzerotti at a time, depending on the size of your pan. Fry for about 2 minutes, until puffed, crisp and golden. Remove with a slotted spoon and drain on paper towels.

Sprinkle the panzerotti with salt flakes and serve immediately.

PIZZETTE FRITTE

FRIED AND STUFFED

 Makes 16 pizzette fritte

plain (all-purpose) flour, for dusting

16 × 50 g (1¾ oz) Fried & sweet dough balls (page 21)

1 litre (1 quart) vegetable oil, for frying

360 g (12½ oz) Marinara sauce (page 22)

400 g (14 oz) fresh mozzarella, sliced or torn

salt flakes, to serve

16 basil leaves

freshly grated Parmigiano Reggiano, to serve (optional)

Preheat the oven to 180°C (350°F) fan-forced, and place a rack on the middle shelf in the oven.

On a lightly floured surface, flatten and roll each dough ball out to a 11.5 cm (4½ in) circle.

In a large saucepan, heat the oil over medium–high heat to 175°C–180°C (345°F–350°F) on a kitchen thermometer.

Carefully fry two to three circles of dough at a time, depending on the size of your pan, for 1–1½ minutes on each side, until puffed, crisp and golden. Remove with tongs or a slotted spoon and drain on paper towels.

Place the pizzette on baking trays and top each with 1½ tablespoons of the marinara sauce and 25 g (1 oz) of the mozzarella. Carefully transfer the trays to the oven and bake for about 2 minutes, just until the mozzarella has melted.

Sprinkle the pizzette with salt flakes and top each with a basil leaf. For an extra cheesy hit, finely grate a little Parmigiano Reggiano on top before serving and enjoy!

PIZZETTE FRITTE with GOAT'S CURD, CHERRY TOMATO & PESTO

FRIED AND STUFFED

 Makes 16 pizzette fritte

plain (all-purpose) flour, for dusting

16 × 50 g (1¾ oz) Fried & sweet dough balls (page 21)

1 litre (1 quart) vegetable oil

250 g (1 cup) Basil pesto (see page 25)

250 g (1 cup) goat's curd

16 cherry tomatoes, halved

freshly grated Parmigiano Reggiano, for sprinkling

salt flakes, to serve

16 basil leaves

On a lightly floured surface, flatten and roll each dough ball out to a 11.5 cm (4½ inch) circle.

In a large saucepan, heat the oil over medium–high heat to 175°C–180°C (345°F–350°F) on a kitchen thermometer.

Carefully fry two to three circles of dough at a time, depending on the size of your pan, for 1–1½ minutes on each side, until puffed, crisp and golden. Remove with tongs or a slotted spoon and drain on paper towels.

Place the pizzette on serving trays and top each with 1 tablespoon of the pesto, 1 tablespoon of the goat's curd, two halves of the tomato and a little Parmigiano Reggiano

To serve, sprinkle salt flakes and pepper over the pizzette, and top each with a basil leaf.

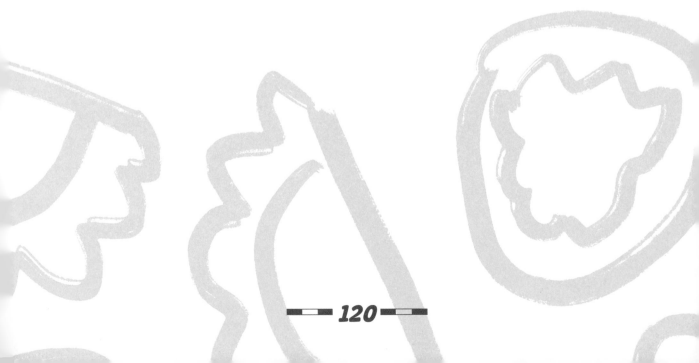

SILVERBEET & THREE CHEESE CALZONE

FRIED AND STUFFED

 Makes 6 calzoni

plain (all-purpose) flour, for
dusting

6 × 130 g (4½ oz) Fried & sweet
dough balls (page 21)

2 tablespoons toasted pine nuts

salt flakes

Marinara sauce (page 22),
to serve

SILVERBEET & THREE CHEESE FILLING

2½ teaspoons extra virgin olive
oil, plus extra for brushing

1 onion, thinly sliced

1 bunch silverbeet (Swiss chard),
leaves stripped and chopped

good pinch of chilli flakes

dash of nutmeg

100 g (3½ oz) ricotta, drained

100 g (3½ oz) goat's cheese

200 g (7 oz) low-moisture
mozzarella, shredded

PARSLEY GARLIC BUTTER

2 teaspoons olive oil

90 g (⅓ cup) salted butter

3 garlic cloves, minced

3 tablespoons finely chopped
parsley leaves

Note: This recipe makes about 80 ml
(⅓ cup). Leftovers will keep for 5–7 days.

Preheat the oven to 220°C (430°F) fan-forced, and place a rack on the middle shelf in the oven. Line two baking trays with baking paper.

To make the filling, heat the oil in a frying pan over medium heat. Add the onion and stir for 1 minute, then add the silverbeet leaves and cook for 2–3 minutes, until the silverbeet is wilted and the onion is cooked through. Stir through the chilli flakes and season with the nutmeg, salt and pepper. Remove from the heat and set aside to cool.

Once cooled, place the silverbeet mixture in a colander and use the back of a spoon to press out the excess liquid. Transfer to a bowl, add the cheeses and mix well. Divide into six portions.

On a lightly floured surface, roll a ball of dough out to a 22 cm (8¾ in) circle, and spoon one portion of the filling over one half of the circle, leaving a 3 cm (1¼ in) border. Sprinkle some of the pine nuts over the filling, then lightly brush the edge of the dough with a little water and fold the dough over to enclose the filling. Press the edges together and crimp to seal. Repeat with the remaining ingredients to make six calzoni.

Place the calzoni on the prepared trays. Use a knife to slice a vent in the top of each calzone for steam to escape, then brush the tops with a little olive oil and sprinkle with salt flakes.

Carefully transfer the trays to the middle rack of the oven and bake the calzoni for 12–15 minutes, until golden brown and baked through.

While the calzoni are baking, prepare the parsley garlic butter. Heat the olive oil, butter and garlic in a small saucepan over medium–low heat and saute for just a few minutes, until fragrant. Do not allow the garlic to brown. Remove from the heat and stir in the parsley. If you make ahead of time, store in an airtight container in the fridge and melt before using (see Note).

Lightly brush the calzoni with the parsley garlic butter, and serve hot with a bowl of marinara sauce on the side for dipping.

ITALIAN SAUSAGE & ROASTED RED PEPPER CALZONE

 Makes 6 calzoni

2½ teaspoons extra virgin olive oil, plus extra for brushing

1 onion, thinly sliced

600 g (1 lb 5 oz) Italian pork sausage, casings removed

200 g (7 oz) marinated roasted red bell peppers (capsicums), drained and sliced

good pinch of chilli flakes

plain (all-purpose) flour, for dusting

6 × 130 g (4½ oz) Fried & sweet dough balls (page 21)

135 g (5 oz) Marinara sauce (see page 22), plus extra to serve

300 g (3 cups) shredded low-moisture mozzarella

salt flakes

Preheat the oven to 220°C (430°F) fan-forced, and place a rack on the middle shelf in the oven. Line two baking trays with baking paper.

Heat the oil in a frying pan over medium heat. Add the onion and stir for 1 minute, then add the sausage, crumbling it into the pan. Break up the sausage using a wooden spoon and cook for 3–4 minutes, until just cooked through. Stir through the bell pepper and chilli flakes, and season with pepper. Remove from the heat, divide into six portions and set aside to cool.

On a lightly floured surface, roll a ball of dough out to form a 22 cm (8¾ in) circle, and spoon 1½ tablespoons of the marinara sauce in the centre, leaving a 3 cm (1¼ in) border.

Use a slotted spoon to allow a little fat to drain from one portion of filling, then place the filling on one half of the dough circle, leaving a 3 cm (1¼ in) border, and sprinkle with some of the mozzarella. Lightly brush the edge of the dough with water, then fold the dough over to enclose the filling. Press the edges together and crimp to seal. Repeat with the remaining ingredients to make six calzoni.

Place the calzoni on the prepared trays. Use a knife to slice a vent in the top of each calzone for steam to escape, then brush the tops with a little olive oil and sprinkle with salt flakes.

Carefully transfer the trays to the middle rack of the oven and bake the calzoni for 12–15 minutes, until golden brown and baked through.

Serve the calzoni hot with a bowl of marinara sauce on the side for dipping.

SWEET GRAPE FOCACCIA

SWEET

 Makes 1 × 23 × 33 cm (9 × 13 in) focaccia

1 × prepared Focaccia dough
(see page 16)

300 g (10½ oz) seedless black
grapes, rinsed, drained and
patted dry

55 g (¼ cup) raw caster
(superfine) sugar

¼ teaspoon fennel seeds

¼ teaspoon aniseed

1 tablespoon extra virgin olive oil

Preheat the oven to 200°C (400°F) fan-forced, and place a rack on the middle shelf in the oven.

Press lightly oiled fingers into the dough to create dimples up and down the entire surface.

Scatter the grapes over the dough, ensuring even coverage. Use your fingers to lightly press the grapes into the dough, then sprinkle over 3 tablespoons of the sugar and all of the fennel and aniseed. Drizzle with the olive oil.

Carefully transfer the focaccia to the middle rack of the oven and bake for 20–25 minutes, until the base is fragrant and golden and the grapes are juicy and bursting.

Place the pan on a wire rack and sprinkle the focaccia with the remaining sugar. Let the focaccia cool slightly before carefully transferring to a chopping board and cutting.

Delicious served hot, warm or at room temperature, and best eaten on the day the focaccia is baked.

CINNAMON SUGAR PIZZETTE FRITTE

SWEET

 Makes 16 pizzette fritte

plain (all-purpose) flour, for dusting

16 × 50 g (1¾ oz) Fried & sweet dough balls (page 21)

1 litre (1 quart) vegetable oil, for frying

CINNAMON SUGAR

110 g (½ cup) caster (superfine) sugar

1½ tablespoons ground cinnamon

¼ teaspoon vanilla bean powder

Note: This cinnamon sugar recipe will make about 110 g (½ cup). Left-over sugar will keep in an airtight container in the pantry for up to 6 months.

To make the cinnamon sugar, place all the ingredients in a jar, seal and shake to combine (see Note).

On a lightly floured surface, flatten and roll or press each dough ball out to an oblong shape, about 20 × 9 cm (8 × 3½ in).

In a large saucepan, heat the oil over medium–high heat to 175°C–180°C (345°F–350°F) on a kitchen thermometer.

Carefully fry two to three pieces of dough at a time, depending on the size of your pan, for 1–1½ minutes on each side, until puffed, crisp and golden. Remove with tongs or a slotted spoon and drain on paper towels.

Toss the pizzette in the cinnamon sugar and serve immediately.

BANANA NUTELLA CALZONE
with MASCARPONE

 Makes 6 calzoni

plain (all-purpose) flour, for dusting

6 × 130 g (4½ oz) Fried & sweet dough balls (page 21)

230 g (¾ cup) Nutella

6 small bananas (about 65 g/2¼ oz each), sliced into 2 cm (¾ in) pieces

180 g (6½ oz) ricotta, drained

2 tablespoons melted salted butter

2 tablespoons raw caster (superfine) sugar

icing (confectioners') sugar, for dusting

30 g (¼ cup) toasted hazelnuts, chopped

FRANGELICO MASCARPONE

125 g (½ cup) mascarpone, chilled

3 tablespoons Frangelico

2 tablespoons icing (confectioners') sugar

Preheat the oven to 220°C (430°F) fan-forced, and place a rack on the middle shelf in the oven. Line two baking trays with baking paper.

On a lightly floured surface, roll a ball of dough out to form a 6 mm (¼ in) thick, 22 cm (8¾ in) circle. Spoon 2 tablespoons of the Nutella over the centre, leaving a 2 cm (¾ in) border. Top with one of the sliced bananas and dollop over 2 tablespoons of the ricotta.

Lightly brush the edge of the dough with a little water, then fold the dough over to enclose the filling. Press the edges together and crimp to seal. Repeat with the remaining ingredients to make six calzoni.

Place the calzoni on the prepared trays. Use a knife to slice a vent in the top of each calzone for steam to escape, then brush the tops with the melted butter and sprinkle with the caster sugar.

Carefully transfer the trays to the middle rack of the oven and bake the calzoni for 12–15 minutes, until golden brown and baked through.

To prepare the Frangelico mascarpone, combine the ingredients in a bowl and whisk together until creamy. Cover and refrigerate until ready to serve.

Finish the calzoni with a dusting of icing sugar, a dollop of the Frangelico mascarpone and a sprinkle of the hazelnuts.

APPLE CINNAMON CALZONE

SWEET

 Makes 6 calzoni

6 × small apples (125 g/4½ oz each), cored and thinly sliced

100 g (3½ oz) brown sugar

1½ teaspoons ground Dutch cinnamon, plus extra to serve

1½ teaspoons vanilla bean paste

2½ teaspoons cornflour (corn starch)

60 g (¼ cup) salted butter, melted

6 × 130 g (4½ oz) Fried & sweet dough (page 21)

plain (all-purpose) flour, for dusting

2 tablespoons raw caster (superfine) sugar

vanilla ice cream, to serve

Preheat the oven to 220°C (430°F) fan-forced, and place a rack on the middle shelf in the oven. Line two baking trays with baking paper.

Combine the apple, brown sugar, cinnamon, vanilla paste, cornflour and half the melted butter in a bowl. Divide into six portions.

On a lightly floured surface, roll a ball of dough out to a 6 mm (¼ in) thick, 22 cm (¾ in) circle. Spoon one portion of the filling over one half of the circle, leaving a 3 cm (1¼ in) border.

Lightly brush the edge of the dough with a little water, then fold the dough over to enclose the filling. Press the edges together and crimp to seal. Repeat with the remaining ingredients to make six calzoni.

Place the calzoni on the prepared trays. Use a knife to slice a vent in the top of each calzone for steam to escape, then brush the tops evenly with the remaining melted butter and sprinkle with the sugar.

Carefully transfer the trays to the middle rack of the oven and bake the calzoni for 12–15 minutes, until golden brown and baked through.

Serve straight from the oven, topped with a dusting of cinnamon and a generous scoop of vanilla ice cream.

INDEX

Published in 2023 by Smith Street Books
Naarm (Melbourne) | Australia
smithstreetbooks.com

ISBN: 978-1-9227-5445-5

Smith Street Books respectfully acknowledges the Wurundjeri People
of the Kulin Nation, who are the Traditional Owners of the land on
which we work, and we pay our respects to their Elders past and present.

Series publisher: Hannah Koelmeyer
Editor: Avery Hayes
Design and illustrations: George Saad
Typesetter: Megan Ellis
Photography: Emily Weaving
Food styling: Deborah Kaloper
Food preparation: Caroline Griffiths and Claire Pietersen
Proofreader: Ariana Klepac
Indexer: Helena Holmgren

Printed & bound in China by C&C Offset Printing Co., Ltd.

Book 272
10 9 8 7 6 5 4 3 2 1